Totally Lent!

A KID'S JOURNEY TO EASTER 2013

Jean Larkin

Pflaum Publishing Group
Dayton, OH

About the Author

Jean Larkin has been writing and editing material for Catholic children and young people for more than thirty years.

Totally Lent! is also available for primary and junior high students. *Totally Lent! A Child's Journey to Easter 2013* and *Totally Lent! A Teen's Journey to Easter 2013* are available from Pflaum Publishing Group.

Edited by Michelle Coffey
Graphic design by Kathryn Cole
Cover illustration by Amy Wummer

Pflaum Publishing Group
2621 Dryden Road, Suite 300
Dayton, OH 45439
800-543-4383
pflaum.com

ISBN 978-1-935042-91-4

Zone in on Lent

When Jesus knew his time to be crucified was drawing near, he went into the desert for forty days. He fasted and prayed. He concentrated totally on making his spirit strong. As you might say today, he was "in the zone."

Lent is time for us to be "in the zone." In union with Jesus, we try to make our spirits stronger. The stronger our spirits get, the more we grow in faith.

Get your head in the game!
Getting strong in spirit requires concentration. It's like getting your "head in the game" or being "in the zone." Right now, concentrate on this rebus and discover another word for paying close attention.

_____

Working Line

Answer: ____ ____ ____ ____ ____

When you see this symbol, go to page 62 and put a small dot in the corresponding space. You'll find out why when Lent is over. Go ahead and do this one now.

K 23

3

Focus on Prayer

During his forty days in the desert, Jesus prayed.

Throughout the Gospels we often see Jesus praying. His spirit grows stronger each time. Prayer makes your faith stronger, too.

During your forty days of Lent, you can pray.

Prayer is important every day of the year, but Lent is a time for extra prayer. Prayer will keep you focused on your faith and on your Lenten journey with Jesus.

Make this prayer personal by filling in the blanks.

My Lenten Prayer

Lord, as I walk with you to Calvary this Lent, I am trying to

_____

_____

as my Lenten sacrifice. Please give me the strength and the will to stick with my intention. By your cross and resurrection, Lord, you have set me free. You are the Savior of the world. Amen.

After you have completed the activity on each page of this book, look for this symbol as a reminder to say your special Lenten prayer each day.

Focus on Fast

During his forty days in the desert, Jesus fasted and abstained.

Fasting has to do with the amount of food you eat. Jesus did a "complete" fast. This means he ate nothing at all. Adult Catholics do a "partial" fast. On Ash Wednesday and Good Friday, they eat only one full meal each day, plus two small meals.

Abstaining has to do with totally doing without something. Catholics who are fourteen or older abstain from eating meat on Ash Wednesday and on the Fridays of Lent.

During your forty days of Lent, you can fast and abstain.

Right now your body is still growing. You need three good meals each day. So you should **NOT** fast by cutting back on your meals. But you **CAN** cut back on foods that are not necessary or that are not good for you.

You can totally give up (abstain from) a special treat. Or you can abstain from a bad habit, like talking back to your parents.

Here are some ideas. Circle those that are NOT necessary or that are NOT good.

Potatoes	Potato chips	Be bossy	Disobey teacher
Sass parents	Make your bed	Cookies	Read books
Bananas	Do dishes	Apples	Argue
Video games	Ice cream	Set table	Eggs
Jelly beans	Candy bars	Soda pop	Gum

Which of these things could you give up during Lent? Or maybe you have a better idea. Write on this line what you plan to do.

_____

40

Ash Wednesday–February 13

Today's Gospel: Matthew 6:1-6, 16-18

Today blessed ashes are pressed on our foreheads in the shape of a cross. We hear one of two short reminders. One reminds us how to live, and the other reminds us how God made us. Start at #1 and write every other letter on the blanks inside the cross. Then start at #2 and write every other letter on the lines below.

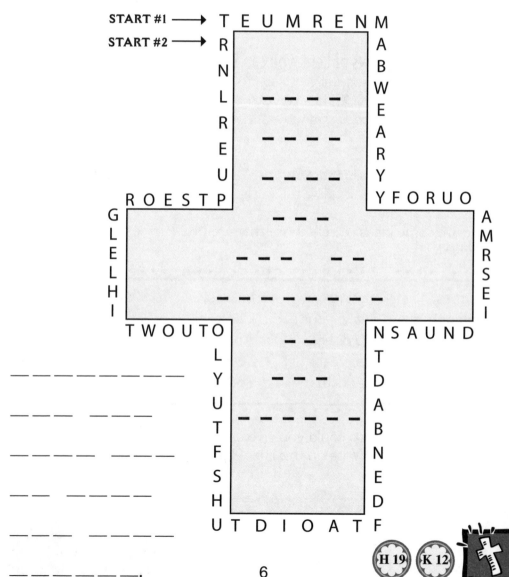

START #1 ⟶

START #2 ⟶

_ _ _ _ _ _ _ _ _ _ _ _ _

_ _ _ _ _ _

_ _ _ _ _ _ _

_ _ _ _ _ _ _

_ _ _ _ _ _ _.

6

Thursday after Ash Wednesday–February 14 · 39

Today's Gospel: Luke 9:22-25

If any want to become my followers, let them deny themselves and take up their cross daily and follow me (9:24).

The message today is not that we all must die on the cross like Jesus. To deny yourself and take up your cross can mean many things. It means caring not only about yourself but also about others. It means bearing your struggles in life with patience and faith. It means recognizing what needs to die within you and what needs to rise, for each time something dies in you that is not good, something rises in you that is better.

Here is a list of some of the things we all need to let die so that better things can rise. To complete each set, fill in the missing letters. Each missing letter is represented by the letter that comes BEFORE it in the alphabet.

1. Let unfairness die so that __ __ __ __ __ __ __ can rise.
   K V T U J D F

2. Let greed die so that __ __ __ __ __ __ __ __ __ __ can rise.
   H F O F S P T J U Z

3. Let grudges die so that __ __ __ __ __ can rise.
   N F S D Z

4. Let selfishness die so that __ __ __ __ __ __ __ can rise.
   T F S W J D F

5. Let falsehoods die so that __ __ __ __ __ can rise.
   U S V U I

6. Let violence die so that __ __ __ __ __ __ __ __ __ __ __ can rise.
   Q F B D F N B L J O H

7. Let boasting die so that __ __ __ __ __ __ __ __ can rise.
   I V N J M J U Z

8. Let cheating die so that __ __ __ __ __ __ __ can rise.
   I P O F T U Z

E 23 L 8

7

Friday after Ash Wednesday–February 15

Today's Gospel: Matthew 9:14-15

John's disciples asked Jesus, "Why do we and the Pharisees fast often, but your disciples do not fast?" (9:14)

"Why do I have to do this? He never has to!" Sound familiar? That's the same complaint John's disciples had for Jesus. Some things never change!

Jesus gave them this example. "The wedding guests cannot mourn as long as the bridegroom is with them, can they? The days will come when the bridegroom is taken away from them, and then they will fast" (9:15).

Think about Jesus' example and answer these questions.

Who was the bridegroom? _____

Who were the guests? _____

To what was Jesus referring when he said, "when the bridegroom is taken away"? _____

_____

Why would the guests fast after that? _____

_____

What message was Jesus trying to get across? _____

_____

H 14 F 8

Today's Gospel: Luke 5:27-32

The Pharisees and scribes complained, "Why do you eat and drink with tax collectors and sinners?" (5:30)

Was Jesus giving everyone a mixed message? He said to live a good life but he ate dinner with people who didn't! Let's look at it a little differently.

A great doctor was asked to come to a village where many people were sick. The doctor went. The leaders of the village were so happy that they threw a great banquet to honor the doctor. But the doctor didn't show up at the banquet. After hours of searching, they found the doctor tending to the sick, trying to help them get better.

The story makes sense, doesn't it? Why should someone who came to help others spend time with people who don't need help?

Here is a "mixed" message of pictures, symbols, and words. Sound them out and decode them to find what Jesus told the Pharisees.

_____

_____

Working Lines

_____

_____

_____

Answer Line

F 13   H 4

Hocus Pocus

Just as Jesus finished his forty days of fast, the devil came to visit him. The devil couldn't stand to see Jesus so full of the Holy Spirit and focused on his Father. So the devil tried some hocus pocus to break his focus!

First, the devil tempted Jesus with food: "If you are God's Son, turn this stone into bread."
Unscramble these words to see what Jesus said to the devil.

NOE SODE TON EVIL YB DABER NOELA

" _____ _____ _____ _____ _____ _____ _____ _____. "

Then the devil tempted Jesus with power and glory. The devil showed Jesus all the kingdoms of the world: "Worship me, and this can all be yours."
Unscramble these words to see what Jesus said to the devil.

SHIPROW HET DROL OYRU OGD DAN VERSE LONY IMH

" _____ _____ _____ _____ _____ _____

_____ _____. "

Finally, the devil tried to get Jesus to test the power of his Father. The devil took Jesus to the pinnacle of the temple in Jerusalem: "If you are really God's Son, jump! God will send angels to save you."
Unscramble these words to see what Jesus said to the devil.

OD TON STET ETH LDRO ROYU GDO

" _____ _____ _____ _____ _____ _____ _____. "

(Based on Luke 4:1-13, the Gospel for the First Sunday of Lent.)

Keep Your Focus

How are you doing with staying focused on Lent? Do you think you could be as strong against temptation as Jesus was? Read each of these possibilities and write how you would answer.

For Lent, you decided to give up *Chocolate Explosion*, your favorite candy bar. You're doing pretty well. Then one day your grandfather comes to visit. He pulls out two *Chocolate Explosions* and says, "Come on! Let's go eat our favorite treat while we watch the game."

What would you say or do?

_____

_____

You and Elaine are both campaigning for the office of class president. You each have to give a speech about why you would like to be elected. A classmate advises you, "Don't try to convince the class that you would be a good president. Just tell them why Elaine would be a lousy president. Talk about how clumsy she is and that she didn't make the debate team, stuff like that."

What would you say or do?

_____

_____

After school on Friday, you go with some friends to a pizza place. You order cheese pizza. Someone turns to you, laughs, and says, "Pretending you're a saint or something?"

What would you say or do?

_____

_____

11

First Monday of Lent–February 18

Today's Gospel: Matthew 25:31-46

"When the Son of Man comes in his glory...then he will sit on the throne of his glory" (25:31).

"He will come again in glory to judge the living and the dead...." You say this sentence every Sunday when you say the creed during Mass. But what really will happen on the last day? Today Jesus answers that question with a story.

Here is part of the story. Sometimes a picture is given instead of a word. See if you can guess the right word for the picture.

When the Son of Man comes with all his 👼, he will sit on his throne of glory. All nations will gather before him. Then he will separate them, as a 🧑 separates his 🐑 from his goats. The 🐑 he will put on his right ✋ and the goats on his left.

The 👑 will say to those on his right, "Come, you are blessed by my Father. You may enter my kingdom. For I was hungry and you gave me 🍔. I was thirsty and you gave me 🥛. I was a stranger and you welcomed me. I was naked and you gave me 👕. I was sick and you took care of me. I was in 🚪 and you visited me."

Then these good people will say to him, "Lord, when was it that we ✏ you hungry and gave you 🍔? **R** thirsty and gave you 🥛? When were you a stranger and we welcomed you? **R** naked and gave you 👕? When were you sick **R** in 🚪 and we visited you?"

And the 👑 will answer them, "Whenever you did it to anyone, you did it to me. ✔ all human beings are members of my 👨‍👩‍👧‍👦."

First Tuesday of Lent–February 19

35

Today's Gospel: Matthew 6:7-15

Pray in this way: Our Father in heaven, hallowed be your name (6:9).

Jesus went on to teach the people the prayer we now call the Lord's Prayer or the Our Father. The words were new to the people then, but today we know them very well.

When you know the words to a prayer, it is easy to slip into saying them automatically without thinking. Jesus warned against praying that way. Decode this message to read Jesus' warning.

Code

= A	‡ = E	= M	= O	= R	= T	= W
/// = D	= H	= N	= P	# = S	= U	= Y

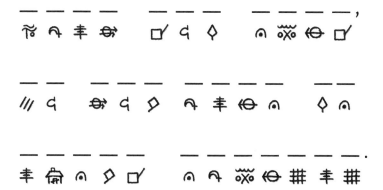

WHEN YOU PRAY,

DO NOT HEAP UP

EMPTY PHRASES.

The next time you say the Lord's Prayer, say it slowly. Think about each phrase and what it means.

First Wednesday of Lent–February 20

Today's Gospel: Luke 11:29-32

This generation is an evil generation; it asks for a sign, but no sign will be given to it except the sign of Jonah (11:29).

Jesus had cured the sick, raised the dead, fed the hungry, and driven out evil spirits. What other sign did these people want? Finally, Jesus told them that the sign Jonah gave many years before was the only sign they were going to get! What sign was Jesus talking about?

Look up the Book of Jonah in your Bible. There are four very short chapters in it. You will find the answers to these questions in the first two chapters.

1. Where did God tell Jonah to go?

_____

2. What was Jonah to do there?

_____

3. What did Jonah do instead?

_____

4. What happened to Jonah?

_____

5. What did the Lord do to save Jonah?

_____

6. How long was it before Jonah finally got to dry land?

_____

7. What did Jonah's story tell people about Jesus?

_____

F 23   M 14

Today's Gospel: Matthew 7:7-12

Ask, and it will be given you; search, and you will find; knock, and the door will be opened for you (7:7).

Wouldn't it be great if what Jesus said meant that we'd get anything we ever prayed for?

Solve this rebus to discover what God is asking you to do when you "ask" but do not "receive."

+ − − **K** =

Working Line

+ **T** − =

Working Line

B + − + **D** =

Working Line

_____ _____ _____

Answer

The Chair of St. Peter–February 22

Today's Gospel: Matthew 16:13-19

You are Peter, and on this rock, I will build my church. I will give you the keys of the kingdom of heaven (16:18-19).

Today we celebrate a special feast that honors not only St. Peter, our first pope, but the role of the pope in the Church. A pope is the shepherd of all the Catholics everywhere in the world.

Each pope has a coat of arms that tells us something about him. Here is Pope Benedict XVI's coat of arms. Color it according to the code.

1 = red
2 = gold or yellow
3 = silver or grey
4 = black
5 = brown

To learn what each element in Pope Benedict's coat of arms stands for, go to www.vatican.va/holy_father/ and click on Benedict XVI. Then click on his coat of arms.

First Saturday of Lent—February 23

31

Today's Gospel: Matthew 5:43-48

Love your enemies (5:44).

These words of Jesus are hard to take. Why couldn't we just *avoid* our enemies? If we didn't strike back at them, wouldn't that be good enough? It is really hard to actually love them.

Begin with the "I" and write down every other letter from around the heart. Find out why Jesus told us to love our enemies.

Start

I 2   E 6

Hocus Pocus?

 took Peter, John, and James up on a to .

 was wearing his robe and sandals and looked like he always did.

Suddenly, his clothes became dazzling white, his face changed, and two great prophets, [image] and [image], were there with him! They were talking to [image] about his departure from the [image].

Peter, John, and James didn't know what to think! Was this some kind of hocus pocus? Were their eyes just out of focus?

Peter said, "[image], it is good for us to be here. Let's make three [image], one for you, one for [image], and one for [image].

Then from a [image] came a voice. "This is my Son; my Chosen; listen to him!" Then [image] was alone again.

Peter, John, and James told no one about this event until after rose from the dead.

(Based on Luke 9:28b-36, the Gospel for the Second Sunday of Lent.)

Out of Focus?

Did you ever see something you just couldn't believe?

What happened on the mountain may have been hard for Peter, John, and James to believe, but it was no trick! Jesus was transformed so the apostles could see the glory of his divinity. The apostles were in awe and wanted to build dwelling places for Jesus and Moses and Elijah so they could stay there, on the mountain, forever.

Here are three tents. On each, write the name of one person in your life you would like to keep with you forever. In the space beside each tent, explain why each person is special to you.

30 Second Monday of Lent—February 25

Today's Gospel: Luke 6:36-38

The amount you give will be the amount you get back (6:38).

Today's Gospel gives us the step-by-step directions to be successful. How we treat others is the way we will be treated. It's simple enough, but we all make mistakes. Sometimes change comes slowly. We take small steps.

Start at the **bottom** of these steps and follow the directions. Make one little change on each step and see where it takes you.

7 Scramble the letters in the new word to create a word for who will give back to us what we give others. _____

6 Change one letter from the new word to create a word for a popular pet. _____

5 Delete one letter from the new word to create a word for a female deer. _____

4 Change one letter in the new word to create a word for a symbol of the Holy Spirit. _____

3 Change one letter in the new word to create a word that completes this sentence: Jesus said, "_____ one another."

2 Change one letter in GIVE to create a word that completes this sentence: We must try to _____ the way Jesus taught us.

Jesus said, *"The amount you give will be the amount you get back."*

Step 7
Step 6
Step 5
Step 4
Step 3
Step 2
Step 1 / **GIVE**

F 6   I 18

Today's Gospel: Matthew 23:1-12

Jesus spoke to the people about the scribes and Pharisees. He said, "Do whatever they teach you and follow it; but do not do as they do" (23:3).

The scribes and Pharisees were teachers of God's laws. Jesus was clear that the people should follow those laws. But he warned against following the teachers' example. When they were judging others, they needed to look in a mirror. And that's a clue for reading the rest of Jesus' message!

Second Wednesday of Lent–February 27

Today's Gospel: Matthew 20:17-28

Whoever wishes to be great among you must be your servant, and whoever wishes to be first among you must be your slave; just as the Son of Man came not to be served but to serve (20:26-27).

Jesus picked each of these men to be his apostle. When they started arguing about who should be first in his kingdom, he corrected them about his real mission. Find the name of each of the twelve apostles in this puzzle. (There were two apostles named James.) When you are finished, go back and write the unused letters on the lines below. They will spell out a hidden message. (You will not need all the letters for the message.)

Andrew
Bartholomew
(sometimes known as Nathanael)
James (son of Alphaeus)
James (son of Zebedee)
John
Judas
Matthew
Peter
Philip
Simon
Thaddaeus
Thomas

T	W	E	H	T	T	A	M	B	H	E
S	I	M	O	N	O	W	N	A	E	C
H	O	S	E	N	T	E	O	R	S	R
J	J	A	M	E	S	R	E	T	U	P
P	O	L	R	A	A	D	C	H	E	I
E	J	H	M	E	J	N	U	O	A	L
D	A	O	N	U	T	A	S	L	D	I
S	H	W	D	A	S	E	M	O	D	H
T	A	A	T	T	M	H	P	M	A	P
I	S	A	S	A	X	P	K	E	H	P
K	F	R	J	N	F	N	N	W	T	L

Today's Gospel: Luke 16:19-31

Jesus told the story of the rich man who ignored the needs of a poor man named Lazarus. After both died, the rich man went to hell and the poor man went to heaven. The rich man begged Father Abraham to let Lazarus give him just one drop of water. When that was denied, he asked that Lazarus be sent to his five brothers while they were alive to warn them to repent. He said, "If someone goes to them from the dead, they will listen." Abraham replied, "If they don't listen to Moses and the prophets, they won't listen to someone who rises from the dead" (16:19-31).

Jesus used this story to teach a lesson to all of us. It's as simple as 1-2-3.

1. Fill in the missing letters in these other lessons Jesus taught us.

F___L___OW   G____   ____'S   LA____S.

L___VE   ____NE   ____   ____O____HE____.

____IVE   ____   ____LP   TO   T____OSE   ____N   N____E____.

2. Write each of the missing letters on this Working Line.

Working Line

3. Rearrange the letters to spell out the lesson Jesus taught us today.
(The first letter in each word is filled in already, so cross those letters off your list.)

D____   G____   ____   ____   W____   ____   ____   ____

O____   E____   ____   ____   ____.

L 23   E 10

23

Second Friday of Lent—March 1

Today's Gospel: Matthew 21:33-43, 45-46

Jesus told the people another story. A man leased his vineyard to tenants. At harvest time he sent servants to collect his produce. But the tenants killed the servants and kept all the produce for themselves. A second time, the man sent servants and they were also killed. Then the man sent his own son, thinking the tenants would respect his son. But they also killed the son. Jesus asked the people, "What do you think the landowner will do to these tenants?" The people all said, "He will kill them and lease to new tenants." But Jesus said, "Have you not read in the scriptures: 'The stone that the builders rejected has become the cornerstone'?" (21:33-42)

World Day of Prayer

To learn what lesson Jesus was teaching with this story, rewrite the following sentence by "rejecting" each letter in each word and replacing it with the letter that comes AFTER it in the alphabet. (Z will be A.)

___ _____ ___ ___ ____ __ _____

SGD JHMFCNL NE FNC VHKK AD SZJDM

____ ____ ___ ___ _____ __ _

ZVZX EQNL XNT ZMC FHUDM SN Z

_____ ____ _____ ___ _____

ODNOKD SGZS OQNCTBDR SGD EQTHSR

___ ____ _____.

NE SGD JHMFCNL

Second Saturday of Lent–March 2

25

Today's Gospel: Luke 15:1-3, 11-32

If you have trouble filling in these blanks, read today's Gospel—the story of the prodigal son—in your Bible.

1. A man had two sons. The _____ son asked for his share of the estate.

2. He went to another country, where he _____ the money foolishly.

3. A severe _____ took place in that country.

4. He got a job feeding _____.

5. He would have gladly eaten the _____ food, but no one gave him anything. He was starving.

6. He decided to go home and ask his father for a _____.

7. His father saw him coming, ran to him, and put his _____ around him.

8. The son said, "Father, I have _____ against heaven and before you. I am no longer _____ to be called your _____."

9. But the father said, "Quick, bring out a robe, and put a ring on his finger and sandals on his feet. Kill the _____ calf and let us _____. This son of mine was _____ and is _____ again. He was _____ and is _____!"

Hocus Pocus

A man found no fruit on a fig tree planted in his vineyard. He said to the gardener, "For three years I have come looking for fruit on this fig tree, and still I find none. Cut it down!"

The gardener pleaded, "Sir, let it alone for one more year. I will dig around it and put manure on it. If it bears fruit next year, well and good; but if not, you can cut it down." The gardener had faith that if the tree was given proper care, it would become healthy.

(Based on Luke 13:1-9, the Gospel for the Third Sunday of Lent.)

If you are like the tree in this story, and a swarm of "locusts" is eating away at your faith, what could you do? For each "locust" on this tree, write on the branches of the tree on the next page what you could do to chase that locust away.

Was It Locusts?

H 22   B 7

24

Third Monday of Lent—March 4

Today's Gospel: Luke 4:24-30

No prophet is accepted in HIS OWN hometown (4:24).

The people of Nazareth knew Jesus as the son of Mary and Joseph. When he claimed he was the Son of God, they found it difficult to believe. Sometimes we can't believe what is right in front of us. Identify what each of these squares means. Remember—the answer is right in front of you.

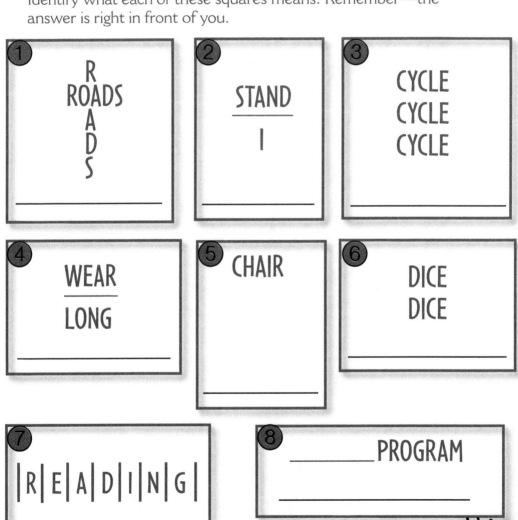

1.
R
ROADS
A
D
S
_____

2.
STAND
―――――
I
_____

3.
CYCLE
CYCLE
CYCLE
_____

4.
WEAR
―――――
LONG
_____

5.
CHAIR
_____

6.
DICE
DICE
_____

7.
|R|E|A|D|I|N|G|
_____

8.
_____PROGRAM
_____

G 23   J 8

28

Third Tuesday of Lent–March 5

23

Today's Gospel: Matthew 18:21-35

Peter asked Jesus how often he should forgive a member of the church who sinned against him. Peter said, "As many as seven times?" Jesus said, "Not seven times, but seventy-seven times" (18:21-22).

If you didn't understand what the number seventy-seven meant to Peter, it might seem that after forgiving someone seventy-seven times, you no longer have to forgive that person anymore. But that isn't what seventy-seven meant to Peter. It meant there was no limit to the number of times to forgive. We must forgive over and over and over again.

Circle each OVER you see in this puzzle. There should be—you guessed it—77! Hint: It helps to use a ruler and a different color ink for each direction.

		O	V	R	R	E	V	O	E			
	O	E	E	E	O	V	E	R	R	V		
	R	V	V	V	V	R	O	V	E	R	O	O
	V	E	O	O	R	O	V	E	R	E	V	O	V	V
R	O	V	E	R	E	E	O	O	V	E	R	V	E	E	E
V	E	O	R	E	V	O	V	E	R	O	V	E	R	O	R
R	O	R	E	V	O	V	E	O	V	E	R	R	E	V	O
E	V	O	V	O	V	E	R	O	V	E	R	E	V	E	V
R	E	V	O	V	E	R	O	V	E	R	E	V	O	R	E
R	R	E	R	V	R	O	E	V	E	E	V	O	V	E	R
E	O	R	V	E	E	R	V	V	E	V	O	V	E	R	O
V	O	V	E	R	V	R	O	E	O	R	O	E	R	V	O
O	V	R	E	V	O	O	V	E	R	E	V	R	E	V	R
	V	R	R	R	O	V	E	R	O	V	E	R	E	E
		E	E	E	R	E	R	E	V	O	R	R	V
			R	V	V	R	O	V	E	R	V	O
				O	O	O	E	O	R	V	O

29

22 Third Wednesday of Lent–March 6

Today's Gospel: Matthew 5:17-19

Do not think that I have come to abolish the law or the prophets; I have come not to abolish but to fulfill (5:17).

The Ten Commandments God gave to Moses were "the law" Jesus was talking about. When Jesus identified the two Great Commandments—love God and love your neighbor—he wasn't replacing the laws God gave Moses. The two Great Commandments represent the spirit behind each of the Ten Commandments.

Decide which of the two Great Commandments is the spirit behind each of the commandments Moses taught. Write a 1 or a 2 in the spaces given.

1. Love God with all your heart, soul, mind, and strength.
2. Love your neighbor as yourself.

Tell the truth. ___

Honor your mother and father. ___

I am your one and only God. ___

Do not be jealous of your neighbor's possessions or spouse. ___

Do not kill. ___

Keep holy the Lord's Day. ___

Do not steal. ___

Use the Lord's name with respect. ___

Be faithful to your spouse. ___

H 2   I 13   D 10

I Love God   **II** Love Your Neighbor

Third Thursday of Lent–March 7

Today's Gospel: Luke 11:14-23

After Jesus cast out a demon from a man who was mute, people said, "He casts out demons by Beelzebul, the ruler of the demons" (11:14-15).

When people accused him of working with the devil, Jesus could have said to himself, "Sometimes you just can't win!" Have you ever felt like that? You do something nice but get criticized for it? Draw a line from the nice action to the criticism you might hear.

Action	Criticism
Pick up litter in classroom	"You can't borrow it!"
Give up the larger part of a candy bar	"You never liked this kind anyway."
Help brother learn to shoot baskets	"Trying to be teacher's pet?"
Compliment friend on new sweater	"You're just showing off."

When someone criticizes your kind action, that shows something is missing from the relationship. This same thing was missing from the people who criticized Jesus. Solve this rebus to find what it was.

T + 🧶 + 🦵 – 📟 – C =

_____

Working line

_____

Answer

Third Friday of Lent—March 8

Today's Gospel: Mark 12:28-34

One of the scribes asked Jesus, "Which commandment is the first of all?" Jesus answered, "You shall love the Lord your God with all your heart, and with all your soul, and with all your mind, and with all your strength. The second is this, 'You shall love your neighbor as yourself'" (12:30-31).

How will you show that you love God today? Write it here.

How will you show that you love your neighbor today? Write it here.

G 7

H 18

Today's Gospel: Luke 18:9-14

Jesus tells a story about two men who go to the temple to pray. One is a Pharisee, an expert on Jewish law. The other is a tax collector. (At that time, many people despised tax collectors because some of them cheated the people.)

The Pharisee stands up and boasts loudly, "God, thank you that I am better than other people, including this tax collector. I fast twice each week, and I give a tenth of my income to the poor." The tax collector, however, stands far off and will not even look up to heaven. He beats his breast and prays, "God, be merciful to me, a sinner."

Jesus ends his story by saying, "The tax collector goes home justified, but the Pharisee will not. All who exalt themselves will be humbled, but all who humble themselves will be exalted."

See if you understand the point Jesus is making with this story. Read each of these statements about the story and decide if it is **True** or **False**.

1. The prayers of rich people do not please God.   T ___ F ___

2. God loves tax collectors more than lawyers.   T ___ F ___

3. Prayer with a proper attitude pleases God.   T ___ F ___

4. People who brag are not loved by God.   T ___ F ___

5. If you are humble, it is okay to cheat people.   T ___ F ___

6. You should pray with your eyes closed.   T ___ F ___

7. Prayers in church are better than prayers at home.   T ___ F ___

8. Being proud of yourself is a sin.   T ___ F ___

Hocus Pocus

Read the Gospel for the Fourth Sunday of Lent, Luke 15:1-3, 11-32, and then take the quiz on this page and the next. Write your answer to each question and keep track of all your "winnings." If you like, make this a game with your family or friends. Even one other person will do. Take turns answering the questions.

BEHIND THE SCENE

$200
How many sons did the man have?

_____

$400
What did one son ask the father?

_____

$600
How did the father respond?

_____

$800
What did the son do then?

_____

$1,000
What did the other son do?

_____

MAKING THE SCENE

$200
Which son asked for his inheritance?

_____

$400
Where did the young man go?

_____

$600
What happened to all his money?

_____

$800
What did he do next?

_____

$1,000
Who helped him when he needed it?

_____

That's Atrocious!

CHANGE IN SCENE

$200
What disaster took place where the young man went?
_____

$400
How did this affect the young man?
_____

$600
How did the man take care of himself?
_____

$800
What kind of work did he do?
_____

$1,000
What did he decide to do?
_____

RETURN TO THE SCENE

$200
Why did he decide to go home?
_____

$400
What was he going to say to his father?
_____

$600
What surprise did he see when he got home?
_____

$800
What did the father order the servants to do?
_____

$1,000
How did the brother feel about this?
_____

Bonus Question

What is the most common name for this story?
_____

I 15   M 12

35

18 Fourth Monday of Lent—March 11

Today's Gospel: John 4:43-54

Go; your son will live (4:50).

Read today's Gospel, then answer each question and write the verse or verses where you found the answer.

1. In what town is Jesus when the official approaches him?
_____ John 4:_____

2. What does the man want Jesus to do? _____
_____
_____ John 4: _____

3. Why does this man think Jesus can help him? _____
_____
_____ John 4: _____

4. What does Jesus say to the man at first? _____
_____
_____ John 4: _____

5. What is the man's reaction once he learns what Jesus did?
_____
_____ John 4: _____

Is there something special you would like to ask of or say to Jesus? Pretend you have just met him on the street where you live. Write here what you would like to say to him.

_____
_____
_____
_____

E 8 I 22

17

Today's Gospel: John 5:1-16

Later Jesus found him in the temple and said to him, "See, you have been made well! Do not sin any more, so that nothing worse happens to you" (5:14-15).

What did Jesus mean when he said, "Do not sin any more, so that nothing worse happens to you"? Solve this puzzle to find out.

A	B	C	D	E	F	G	H	I	J	K	L	M
1	2	3	4	5	6	7	8	9	10	11	12	13

N	O	P	Q	R	S	T	U	V	W	X	Y	Z
14	15	16	17	18	19	20	21	22	23	24	25	26

23	8	5	14	25	15	21	19	9	14	25	15	21

13	15	22	5	1	23	1	25	6	18	15	13	7

15	4	20	8	1	20	9	19	13	21	3	8	23

15	18	19	5	20	8	1	14	16	8	25	19	9

3	1	12	9	12	12	14	5	19	19

F 10   J 23

Fourth Wednesday of Lent–March 13

Today's Gospel: John 5:17-30

"Very truly, I tell you, the Son can do nothing on his own, but only what he sees the Father doing; for whatever the Father does, the Son does like-wise" (5:19).

If today's Gospel were given a title, it would probably be "Like father, like son." Remember yesterday's Gospel? Some Jewish leaders got angry because Jesus cured a man on the Sabbath. Today, Jesus tells them why he did it.

In just a few words, Jesus tells them:
† God is his Father.
† His power to heal comes from his Father.
† His desire to help people comes from his Father.
† In all that he does, he imitates his Father.
† His Father loves and helps people every single day of the week.
† Jesus, too, loves and helps people every single day of the week.

1. Choose a parent or any other grown-up. Think of the good things that person does for family, friends, and neighbors. For example, maybe that person always listens. Or maybe that person usually cooks supper. List his or her good deeds here.

a) _____

b) _____

c) _____

d) _____

e) _____

f) _____

2. Now put an X beside each good deed that you plan to do when you are grown up.

3. Which of these good deeds can you begin doing now? Put a second X beside each of those things. Do them as often as you can.

Today's Gospel: John 5:31-47

You search the scriptures because you think that in them you have eternal life; and it is they that testify on my behalf. Yet you refuse to come to me to have life (5:39-40).

The Jewish leaders spent hours poring over the Scriptures. Yet they were missing something important about Jesus.

To figure out the names or phrases on some license plates, you have to guess what letters are missing. What are these license plates telling us about who Jesus is? Write the names for Jesus on the lines.

GEEZ-UZ	MS-I-UH
_____	_____
SAYVYR	LMUV-GD
_____	_____
REE-DMR	GUD-SHPRD
_____	_____
SNUV-GD	EMNYUL
_____	_____

D 14

E 11

L 12

14 Fourth Friday of Lent—March 15

Today's Gospel: John 7:1-2, 10, 25-30

He [Jesus] did not wish to go about in Judea because the Jews were looking for an opportunity to kill him (7:1).

Very important: The "Jews" means "some of the Jewish leaders." It does not mean "all Jews." Jesus himself was a Jew, and so were nearly all his friends and followers.

During the next two weeks of Lent, you will be hearing more about the Jews who wanted to kill Jesus. In today's Gospel, they tried to arrest Jesus, but "no one laid hands on him, because his hour had not yet come" (7:30). "His hour" means the hour of Jesus' death on the cross. He knew it was coming. But he knew it would come only in God's good time.

There is a right time for everything. On these clock faces, draw hands that show the right time for you to do each thing on any given Friday.

Wake up

Eat Breakfast

Get to school

Eat Lunch

Arrive home

Eat Dinner

Evening Activity

Pray night prayers

L 6   K 10

40

Fourth Saturday of Lent–March 16

13

Today's Gospel: John 7:40-53

Surely the Messiah does not come from Galilee, does he? Has not the scripture said that the Messiah is descended from David and comes from Bethlehem, the village where David lived? (7:41-42)

When you read the Gospels, it helps to know a bit about the geography of the land where Jesus spent most of his life. Jesus lived, preached, suffered, and died in Galilee, Samaria, and Judea. These three areas were all part of Palestine, which was part of the Roman Empire.

Using this map and what you know about Jesus, explain one important detail about him that the Pharisees didn't know.

_____

_____

_____

_____

_____

_____

_____

_____

_____

GALILEE

Lake Huleh

Chorazin
Mt. of the BEATITUDES
Capernaum — Bethsaida
Cana — Magdala
Mt. CARMEL — Sepphoris — Tiberias — Sea of Galilee
Nazareth

JEZREEL VALLEY — Mt. TABOR

Nain

Caesarea

Mediterranean Sea

SAMARIA

Sebaste (Samaria) — Mt. EBAL — Sychar
Mt. GERIZIM

River Jordan

Jamnia

Emmaus — Jericho
Jerusalem — Bethany
Qumran
Bethlehem

JUDEA

Hebron — Dead Sea

Roman Cities
Jewish Villages

L 11 H 7 I 12

Hocus Pocus

Jesus was teaching in the Temple when the scribes and Pharisees brought a woman and made her stand in front of him. "She has been caught in a terrible sin. She has been unfaithful to her husband. The law of Moses says we should stone her to death. What do you say?"

They were trying to trick Jesus into telling them to break one of the laws of Moses, but Jesus wasn't going to fall for that. He bent down and started writing with his finger in the dirt on the ground.

We don't know for sure what Jesus wrote, but it is said he was writing the sins that the Pharisees and scribes had already committed in their lives. Whether or not that is true, we do know what Jesus said when he stood up.

See if you can read his words upside down. If you can't, just turn the book around.

(Based on John 8:1-11, the Gospel for the Fifth Sunday of Lent.)

Is This Charge Bogus?

When you hear this story about the unfaithful woman who is about to be stoned, you might wonder what it has to do with you or even with anyone else today. Stoning is no longer a form of punishment in our country.

But this story is not about stoning. It is about those who judge others while not admitting their own sinfulness. Most of all, the story is about forgiveness.

When Jesus challenged any of the men to throw a stone if he was himself sinless, not one of them picked up a stone. They knew they had committed sins just as the woman brought before them had.

Do you remember what happened after all the men left and it was only the woman standing there with Jesus? He asked her if anyone was left to condemn her. She replied, "No one, sir." Jesus said, "Neither do I condemn you."

Use the words written on the stones in this pile and put them in the correct order to read what Jesus told her next.

____ ____ ____ , ____ ____ ____

____ ____ ____ ____ ____ .

Fifth Monday of Lent—March 18

Today's Gospel: John 8:12-20

Jesus spoke to the Pharisees."You judge by human standards; I judge no one. Yet even if I do judge, my judgment is valid; for it is not I alone who judge, but I and the Father who sent me" (8:15-16).

Later, the Pharisees ask Jesus, "Where is your Father?" In the following response from Jesus, there are numbers in place of 27 missing letters. Replace each number with the correct letter to reveal Jesus' reply to the Pharisees. (No key is needed.)

Y 1 2   K N 3 W   N 4 5 T H 6 R   M 7

__ ___ _____ __

N 8 R   M 9   F 10 T H 11 R.   12 F   Y 13 14

___ __ _____. __ ___

K N 15 W   M 16,   Y 17 18   W 19 20 21 D

____ ___, ____ _____

K N 22 W   M 23   F 24 T H 25 R   26 L S 27.

____ ___ _____.

Solemnity of St. Joseph—March 19

Today's Gospel: Matthew 1:16, 18-21, 24a

From the record of the genealogy of Jesus, we learn about Joseph, the husband of Mary, of whom Jesus was born, who is called the Messiah (1:16).

There are many legends about St. Joseph, but the only **facts** we have about him are from the Gospels. Look up these passages and summarize each one.

Matthew 1:18-25

_____

Matthew 2:13-15

_____

Matthew 2:19-23

_____

Luke 2:41-51

_____

Now that you know the facts about St. Joseph, circle words from this list that you believe would describe him.

loyal	determined	rich
old	cowardly	strong
faithful	skilled	young
kind	poor	bossy
weak	protective	brave

In your opinion, what makes St. Joseph a good role model?

_____

Fifth Wednesday of Lent–March 20

Today's Gospel: John 8:31-42

Everyone who commits sin is a slave to sin (8:34).

What does it mean to be a slave to sin? Read each of these situations and circle the answer that could make you a slave to sin.

You tell a lie about your friend. Your friend asks you, "Did you say that about me?"
You answer...
     a. "Yes, and I'm sorry."
     b. "No, I did not say that."
Explain how this answer could make you a slave to sin.

You are angry at your mother. Behind her back, you stick out your tongue at her. She turns and asks you, "What did you just do?"
You answer...
     a. "Nothing."
     b. "I stuck out my tongue, and I'm sorry."
Explain how this answer could make you a slave to sin.

On the playground at school, you see two classmates arguing, and one pushes the other. Pretty soon, they are on the ground wrestling and punching each other. The other kids gather around to watch.
You...
     a. watch with the other kids.
     b. get a teacher to stop the fight.
Explain how this answer could make you a slave to sin.

Fifth Thursday of Lent–March 21

Today's Gospel: John 8:51-59

"Very truly, I tell you, whoever keeps my word will never see death" (8:51).

In Jesus' time, one thing you never did was say something against Abraham. Abraham was revered as the father of the Jewish people.

So, the crowd reminded Jesus that Abraham had died. Did Jesus think he was greater than Abraham? When Jesus answered truthfully and said he _was_, the crowd got very angry and tried to stone him to death. But he got away and hid in the temple.

Do you ever get upset? Beside each item below, write 1 if that event would not bother you at all, 2 if it would bother you a little, and 3 if it would bother you a lot.

___ Someone tries to steal your bike.

___ Someone yells, "Your mother's ugly."

___ Someone tries to burn your country's flag.

___ Someone toilet papers your house.

___ Someone starts punching your sister.

___ Someone puts you down for being the "wrong" nationality or color.

___ Someone yells, "You're an idiot!"

When we get upset, we need to ask ourselves, what if I'm wrong? What if there's something here that I don't understand?

Fifth Friday of Lent—March 22

Today's Gospel: John 10:31-42

Jesus again told the people that he was God's Son. Then he said, "If I do the works of my Father, even though you do not believe me, believe the works, so that you may know and understand that the Father is in me and I am in the Father" (10:38).

What were some of the works of the Father that Jesus did? List three.

1. _____

2. _____

3. _____

Jesus taught that people would know his followers by their good works. What three good works can you do to show you follow Jesus?

1. _____

2. _____

3. _____

48

Fifth Saturday of Lent—March 23

Today's Gospel: John 11:45-56

Some of the Jews began believing in Jesus. This worried the Pharisees, who began plotting to kill Jesus. So Jesus went to a town near the wilderness. When Passover was near, his disciples wondered, "Surely he will not come to the festival, will he?" (11:48, 53-56)

The Passover feast commemorated a special event in Jewish history. After the Jews had been enslaved in Egypt for many years, the Lord told Moses to go to Pharaoh and tell him to let the Jews go free. Pharaoh refused. Even after the Lord sent plague after plague upon the land, Pharaoh still refused to let the people go. Finally, the Lord planned to send one last plague on the land. He gave Moses instructions on what to tell the Jews to do so that this last plague would "pass over" them.

You can find the answers to these questions about the first Passover in Exodus 12:1-28.

1. What animal was to be slaughtered and shared by the Jews?

_____

2. What were the Jews to put on their doorposts and lintels?

_____

3. What purpose was this to serve?

_____

4. For how many years were the Jews to celebrate this event?

_____

Bonus Question
When does Passover begin this year? _____

Ups and Downs

This Sunday begins the holiest week of our Church year. It begins on a joyous note. But it is a week of ups and downs. This Sunday even has two names—Passion Sunday and Palm Sunday.

Passion/Palm Sunday

On this day, the people greet Jesus as he rides into Jerusalem. The people cheer "Hosanna" and wave palms in honor of him.

We process around the church on Palm Sunday. We carry and wave palms. We remember the day Jesus is greeted with joy into the city he loves. We sing joyful songs.

On this same day, we hear the story of the rest of the week, which is not happy at all. The story we hear is called the Passion of Our Lord. It tells us of the last days Jesus spends on this earth.

Monday, Tuesday, and Wednesday

In our Gospel readings, we carry a sense of anticipation of the tragic days ahead when Jesus suffers and dies.

On Monday, Jesus visits his friends in Bethany—Mary, Martha, and Lazarus. It is there that Mary anoints Jesus with expensive perfumed oil.

On Tuesday, Jesus talks with his apostles and warns them that one of them will betray him.

On Wednesday, Judas turns Jesus over to be arrested.

Downs and Ups

What do these words have in common? _____

Tricycle	Triathlon	Trifocal	Trio
Triangle	Triplet	Trifold	Tripod
Trinity	Triceps	Trilogy	Tristate

The Triduum

If you answered that all of these words share the prefix *tri*, and it means "three," you are correct! The word *Triduum* means "three days," and they are three very special days in Holy Week. Beginning with the Mass of the Lord's Supper on Holy Thursday evening and lasting through evening prayer on Easter Sunday, the Church celebrates these three most solemn days of the year.

Holy Thursday

Jesus institutes the Eucharist at his last supper with his disciples.

Good Friday

Jesus is crucified and dies. His disciples lay his body in a tomb and use a heavy rock to seal the entrance.

Holy Saturday

At the Easter Vigil we welcome new members to the Church. There are Baptisms, First Communions, and sometimes, Confirmations.

Do you know someone who is becoming a member of the Catholic Church this year? If so, be sure to welcome and congratulate the new member with a card or phone call.

6 Monday of Holy Week—March 25

Today's Gospel: John 12:1-11

You always have the poor with you, but you do not always have me (12:8).

Learn what happened when Jesus' friend Mary anointed him. Fill in the blanks with words from today's Gospel. Then read down the blue highlighted letters to see what the anointing showed Jesus.

Followers of Jesus   _ _ _ _ _ _ _ _ _

The ____ will always be with us.   _ _ _ _

The upcoming feast in Jerusalem   _ _ _ _ _ _ _ _

The town where the dinner was held   _ _ _ _ _ _ _

The brother of Mary   _ _ _ _ _ _ _

The perfumed oil cost 300 _____.   _ _ _ _ _ _

_____ criticized Mary.   _ _ _ _ _

Mary's sister   _ _ _ _ _ _

**The _____ came to see Jesus
and Mary's brother**   _ _ _ _

**The apostle who criticized
Mary kept the common ____.**   _ _ _ _ _

The amount of perfumed oil Mary had   _ _ _ _ _

Mary anointed Jesus' _____.   _ _ _ _

**The oil filled the house
with _____.**   _ _ _ _ _ _ _ _

**The chief _____ planned to
kill Lazarus as well as Jesus.**   _ _ _ _ _ _ _

Tuesday of Holy Week–March 26

5

Today's Gospel: John 13:21-33, 36-38

Where I am going, you cannot follow me now; but you will follow afterward (13:36).

Follow this path to discover what happened after Jesus said this.

e → e → t → i → m → e
r ← h   t   m ← y   d   s   w ← u   y ← s ← w
s → s → a   t ← e   n   i   o   y   c   o
s → u   i   e   l ← l   o   c   c   r
e ← J   i → d → B   f   r   e   h → e   c → o   k   t ← o → n
i → f   u   o ← y   e   o   t   o   y   o   f   l
y → l   f → o → r   i ← w ← l ← w   n   o   w ← l   c   n
m   w   y ← a   t → e   a → i   u   o   d   h   a
n   o ← d   l ← l ← l   e   P   r → s   d   L   r   w   y

Start

———— —— ————, " —————, ———
—— —— ——— ——— ———
———? — —— ——— ———
—— ———— ———— ———."
————— —————," "————————
——— ——— ——— ——— ———
————.""

Wednesday of Holy Week–March 27

Today's Gospel: Matthew 26:14-25

One of the twelve, who was called Judas Iscariot, went to the chief priests and said, "What will you give me if I betray him to you?" (26:14-15)

To learn what the chief priests paid Judas to betray Jesus, complete this puzzle. The number 1 is already in place within Circles A, B, and C. Decide which two other numbers are needed to make all three numbers in each circle equal 10. You may use only the numbers 2 through 7 one time each.

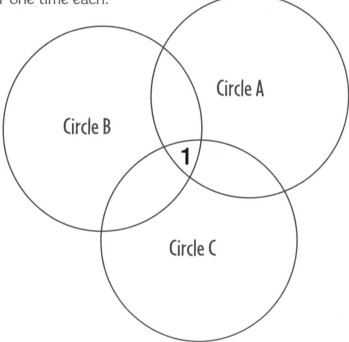

What is the total of the three circles after you have added the numbers? _____

That is the number of silver pieces Judas was paid to betray Jesus.

Holy Thursday—March 28

Today's Gospel: John 13:1-15

If I, your Lord and Teacher, have washed your feet, you also ought to wash one another's feet (13:14).

In Jesus' day, washing feet was a natural thing to do before eating a meal. People walked everywhere in sandals on dusty roads, and their feet got very dirty. But a person considered the leader or the most respected in the group did not usually do the washing. Jesus made the washing of his disciples' feet a symbol of serving others.

At tonight's Mass you will see the priest wash the feet of others in memory of what Jesus did at the Last Supper. It is a reminder to all of us that we, too, must "wash the feet of others." When we help those who need it, we wash their feet. When we are kind to others, we wash their feet. There are many ways to wash the feet of others.

Think of how you can wash someone's feet in the next couple of days. Make a list of ideas so that when a chance comes along, you will recognize it.

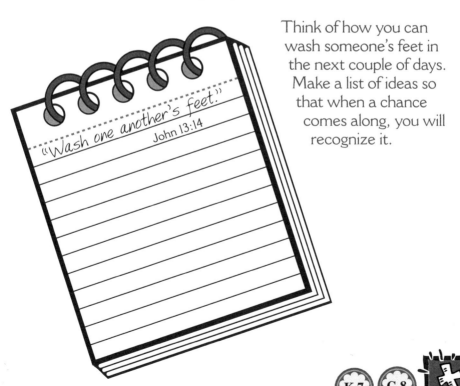

"Wash one another's feet!"
John 13:14

Good Friday–March 29

Today's Gospel: John 18:1—19:42

Jerusalem was a walled city. People entered and exited through gates in the wall. Draw the path you think Jesus took from the time he left the Upper Room until his death. Mark each site with the corresponding number in the text. As you go from one "station" to the next, say this prayer: *Jesus, Son of God, you are my Lord and Savior.*

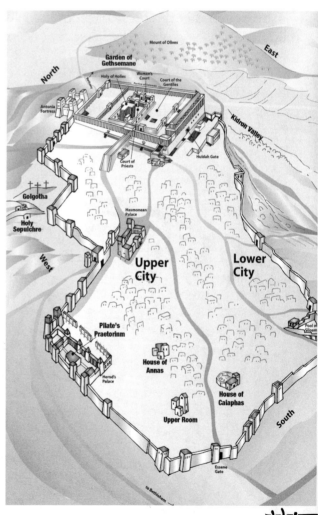

From the **Upper Room**[1], Jesus went out of the city and across the Kidron Valley to the **Garden of Gethsemane**[2] (18:12).

After Jesus' arrest, he was taken to **Annas**[3], the father-in-law of Caiaphas, the high priest who had persuaded the other Jewish leaders to have Jesus killed (18:13).

Annas sent Jesus to **Caiaphas**[4] (18:24).

Caiaphas sent Jesus to **Pilate**[5] (18:28).

Pilate ordered Jesus scourged and put to death to satisfy the people. Jesus carried his cross to **Golgotha**[6], where he was crucified (19:16-18).

After Jesus died, his friends and family prepared his body for burial and placed him in a tomb, now called the **Holy Sepulchre**[7] (18:1).

I 10   N 8

Holy Saturday–March 30

Saturday was the Sabbath for the Jews (and still is). Usually the Sabbath was a calm day set aside to worship God and to rest. But this Sabbath, the day after Jesus died, was different for the Jews who had followed Jesus. They spent the day hiding in fear.

We usually spend this day feeling pretty fine and making preparations to celebrate Easter. Why is this day different for us than it was for the early Christians?

Shade every other box in this grid with a highlighter in checkerboard fashion. On the lines below the grid, write the letters in the highlighted boxes. Then continue with the letters in the last two rows of boxes with no highlights.

The message you find will tell you what we know that the early Christians did not know.

W	R	E	O	K	M	N	T	O	H
E	W	D	T	E	H	A	A	D	T
J	T	E	H	S	E	U	Y	S	D
I	R	D	O	N	S	O	E	T	F

_____

_____

_____

_____

H 9   I 6

Tic-Tac-True?

Do you ever win at Tic-Tac-Toe? If you know the correct answers to these true-or-false questions, you can win. Follow the directions for each answer you pick. Use the grid on the next page.

1. There are four weeks in Lent.
   True? Put an O in square 1.
   False? Put an X in square 1.

2. Catholics 14 and older abstain from meat on Ash Wednesday.
   True? Put an O in square 2.
   False? Put an X in square 2.

3. The ashes put on our foreheads come from burned palms.
   True? Put an O in square 3.
   False? Put an X in square 3.

4. Lent begins on the last Sunday of February each year.
   True? Put an O in square 4.
   False? Put an X in square 4.

5. Jesus spent forty days praying with his disciples in the desert.
   True? Put an O in square 5.
   False? Put an X in square 5.

6. Good Friday is not a holy day of obligation.
   True? Put an O in square 6.
   False? Put an X in square 6.

7. Jesus instituted the Eucharist on the night Passover began.
   True? Put an O in square 7.
   False? Put an X in square 7.

8. The Stations of the Cross remind us of Jesus' suffering and death.
   True? Put an O in square 8.
   False? Put an X in square 8.

9. Herod ordered Jesus' crucifixion.
   True? Put an O in square 9.
   False? Put an X in square 9.

Tic-Tac-False?

1	2	3
4	5	6
7	8	9

H 5   I 8   J 7

0 Easter Sunday—March 31

Today's Gospel: John 20:1-9

A Year Without Easter

Easter is the greatest day of the year for Christians. In fact, if there had been no Easter, there would be no Christians. Our lives would be very different. On this page and the next, put a line through all the events of the coming year that we Catholic Christians would NOT celebrate if there had been no Easter.

2013 Dates

Jan 1:   Mary, Mother of God
          New Year's Day
Jan 6:   Epiphany
Jan 21:   Martin Luther King,
          Jr., Day

Feb 2:   Presentation of the Lord
Feb 10:   Chinese New Year
Feb 12:   Lincoln's Birthday
Feb 13:   Ash Wednesday
Feb 14:   Valentine's Day
Feb 18:   Presidents' Day

Mar 1:   World Day of Prayer
Mar 10:   Daylight Saving Time
          begins
Mar 17:   St. Patrick's Day
Mar 20:   Spring begins
Mar 24:   Palm Sunday
Mar 25:   Passover begins
          at sunset
Mar 28:   Holy Thursday
Mar 29:   Good Friday
Mar 30:   Holy Saturday
Mar 31:   Easter

April 7: Holocaust Remembrance
April 8: Annunciation of the Lord
          (ordinarily celebrated on
          March 25; transferred
          due to Holy Week)
April 22: Earth Day

2013 Dates

May 1:   St. Joseph, the Worker

May 5:   Cinco de Mayo

May 9:   Ascension of the Lord

May 12: Mothers' Day

May 18: Armed Forces Day

May 19: Pentecost

May 26: Trinity Sunday

May 27: Memorial Day

May 31: Visitation of Mary

June 2: Body and Blood
of Christ

June 14: Flag Day

June 16: Fathers' Day

June 21: Summer begins

July 4:   Independence Day

Aug 6:   The Transfiguration

Aug 15: The Assumption

Sept 2: Labor Day

Sept 4: Rosh Hashanah
begins at sunset

Sept 13: Yom Kippur begins
at sunset

Sept 15: Catechetical Sunday

Sept 22: Autumn begins

Oct 14: Columbus Day

Oct 24: United Nations Day

Oct 31: Halloween

Nov 1:   All Saints' Day

Nov 2:   All Souls' Day
Election Day

Nov 3:   Daylight Saving Time ends

Nov 5:   Election Day

Nov 11: Veterans Day

Nov 24: Christ the King

Nov 27: Hanukkah
begins at sunset

Nov 28: Thanksgiving Day

Dec 7:   Pearl Harbor
Remembrance Day

Dec 12: Our Lady of Guadalupe

Dec 21: Winter begins

Dec 25: Christmas Day

Dec 26: Kwanzaa begins

Dec 29: Holy Family

Dec 31: New Year's Eve

Easter Gridlock

To unlock the grid, fill in each space that has a dot in it.

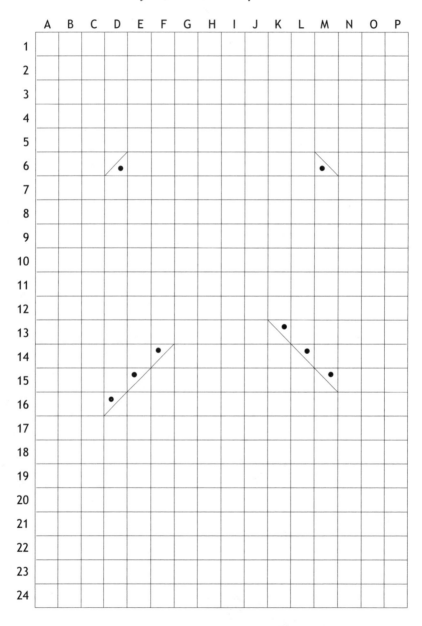

Answers

Page 3: FOX - X + C + BUS - B = FOCUS

Page 6: 1. Turn away from sin and be faithful to the Gospel. 2. Remember you are dust and to dust you will return.

Page 7: 1. justice; 2. generosity; 3. mercy; 4. service; 5. truth; 6. peacemaking; 7. humility; 8. honesty

Page 8: Jesus = bridegroom; Jesus' disciples = guests; Jesus was referring to his own death; the guests would fast from sorrow; Jesus' disciples would fast after he was taken from them.

Page 9: I have come not to call good people but to call sinners.

Page 10: One does not live by bread alone. Worship the Lord your God and serve only him. Do not test the Lord your God.

Page 13: When you pray, do not heap up empty phrases.

Page 14: 1. Ninevah; 2. convert the people; 3. boarded a ship for Tarshish; 4. he was thrown overboard; 5. had him swallowed by a large fish; 6. three days and three nights; 7. Jesus would rise from the dead after three days.

Page 15: TRUCK + STAR – CAR – K = TRUST, RAIN + T – RAT = IN

B + GOAT – BAT + D = GOD

Rebus answer: TRUST IN GOD

Page 17: If you love those who hate you, you love as God loves.

Page 20: GIVE, LIVE, LOVE, DOVE, DOE, DOG, GOD

Page 21: Practice what you preach.

Page 22:

Message: The one chosen to replace Judas was Matthias.

Page 23: Follow God's laws. Love one another. Give help to those in need. Do good while on earth.

Page 24: The kingdom of God will be taken away from you and given to a people that produces the fruits of the kingdom.

Page 25: 1. younger; 2. squandered (or spent); 3. famine; 4. pigs; 5. pigs'; 6. job; 7. arms; 8. sinned, worthy, son; 9. fatted, celebrate, dead, alive, lost, found

Page 28: 1. crossroads; 2. I understand; 3. tricycle; 4. long underwear; 5. high chair; 6. paradise; 7. reading between the lines; 8. space program

Page 29:

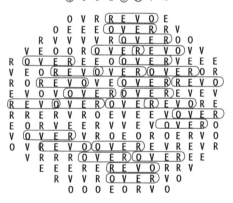

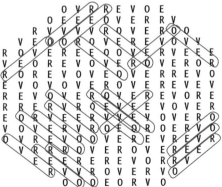

Answers (continued)

Page 30: Answers in this order: 2, 2, 1, 2, 2, 1, 2, 1, 2

Page 31: T + RUGS + CAST – GAS – C = TRUST

Page 33: All are false except #3

Page 34: Behind the Scene: $200-two, $400-for his share of his father's property, $600-divided his property between his two sons, $800-took all he had and left home, $1,000-stayed at home and worked

Making the Scene: $200-the younger son, $400-to a distant country, $600-He spent all his money foolishly. $800-He behaved immorally. $1,000-No one helped him.

Page 35: Change in Scene: $200-a famine, $400-He was dying of hunger. $600-He got a job. $800-He took care of pigs. $1,000-He decided to go home. **Return to the Scene:** $200-He realized his father's workers were better off than he was. $400-He was going to admit that he had been wrong and ask his father for a job. $600-He was surprised to see his father waiting to hug him. $800-The father asked his servants to bring his son clothes and to prepare a celebration meal. $1,000-The older brother was angry. *Bonus Question:* The Prodigal Son

Page 36: 1. Cana, verse 46; 2. Go to Capernaum and heal the man's son, verse 47; 3. He had heard about all Jesus did at the Passover festival, verse 45; 4. "Unless you see signs and wonders you will not believe.", verse 48; 5. He (and his whole household) believed in Jesus, verse 53

Page 37: When you sin, you move away from God. That is much worse than physical illness.

Page 39: Jesus, Messiah, Savior, Lamb of God, Redeemer, Good Shepherd, Son of God, Emmanuel

Page 41: Jesus grew up in Nazareth in Galilee but was born in Bethlehem, which is in Judea.

Page 43: Go your way, and from now on do not sin again.

Page 44: You know neither me nor my Father. If you knew me, you would know my Father also.

Page 49: 1. one-year-old male goat or sheep; 2. the animal's blood; 3. sign to the Lord to skip that house; 4. throughout the generations *Bonus Question:* sundown on March 25, 2013

Page 52: Missing words are: disciples, poor, Passover, Bethany, Lazarus, denarii, Judas, Martha, Jews, purse, pound, feet, fragrance, and priests. Answer: LOVE AND RESPECT

Page 53: Peter said, "Lord, why can I not follow you now? I will lay down my life for you." Jesus said, "Before the cock crows you will deny me three times."

Page 54: 2 + 7, 3 + 6, 4 + 5, 30 pieces of silver

Page 57: We know that Jesus rose from the dead. They did not.

Page 58: True: 2, 3, 6, 7, and 8 False: 1, 4, 5, and 9

Page 59: If all answers are correct, Tic-Tac-Toe is a diagonal line from square 1 to square 9.